Millie Marotta's
Animal
Kingdom

First published in the United Kingdom in 2020 by
Batsford
43 Great Ormond Street
London
WC1N 3HZ
United Kingdom

An imprint of B. T. Batsford Holdings Limited

ISBN 978 1 84994 590 5

A CIP catalogue record for this book is available
from the British Library.

20 19 18 17 16 15 14 13 12 11 10 9 8 7
30 29 28 27 26 25 24

Reproduction by Mission Productions Ltd, Hong Kong
Printed and bound by Toppan Leefung Printing Ltd, China

Millie Marotta's
Animal Kingdom

pocket colouring

BATSFORD

Introduction

I grew up on a smallholding in rural west Wales and it is there that I would say my obsession with all things flora and fauna first began. All those years spent in the countryside, very much immersed in nature, firmly cemented my fascination with the natural world. My favourite pastimes would usually involve either some element of drawing, painting – and generally making a bit of a mess – or playing outside with any one of the many family pets. Imagine my delight when later on I discovered that I could study Wildlife and Illustration together, which is what I went on to do. When I look back now I suppose my path was always mapped out, though I didn't realize it at the time.

I have always been in awe of animals in all their glorious forms – from tiny beetles creeping about beneath leaves in the back garden to the elaborate birds of paradise found in the canopies of tropical rainforests. The captivating charm of the natural world is what brings me back to drawing animals time and time again – it is bursting with an extraordinary array of visual treats.

This book brings together a collection of enchanting fish, birds, mammals, reptiles, invertebrates and amphibians. Although this is ultimately a book of animals, you will also find some plants, trees and flowers included in its pages, among which you may discover the odd bug hiding out. It is a celebration of the animal kingdom as much as it is a colouring and doodle book, waiting for you to lose yourself among the pages.

My illustrations usually begin as quite simple but realistic drawings of the creature. I keep the general form of the animal relatively true to life, but will then begin to elaborate with lots of intricate patterning and detail.

All the drawings in this book begin in black and white. Some might remain so, while others will be flooded with colour. Some will invite you to be even more adventurous and join in by adding your own patterns and textures. These choices are yours to make. On some pages you will find areas of the illustrations have been left empty, crying out for you to embellish in any way you wish. You may choose not to add any colour at all to some and instead just add your own doodles to decorate the animal or add drawings to create a fantastic habitat for the creature. All the drawings in this book were created using a Rotring Rapidograph fine liner, which I use for almost all my work. You can use any pen you choose when it comes to adding your own details to the pages. The finer the pen, the more detail you will be able to add.

For adding colour, I would suggest using coloured pencils rather than felt pens as they are more versatile, allowing you the ability to blend colours and add shading if you wish. You may find some parts of certain drawings are too detailed to colour in every tiny little section, and so you may choose to simply colour over the top of these areas, allowing the textures and patterns underneath to show through.

At the end of the book you will find a few empty pages waiting to be brought to life by you. You might want to try making a copy of your favourite illustrations from the book, or you may be feeling confident enough to draw something entirely your own. Whatever you decide to include on these pages they are there for you to fill with your own animal kingdom. The important thing is that while this may be a book of my drawings to begin with, by the time you have finished, you will have made it your own and it will be uniquely yours.

Millie Marotta

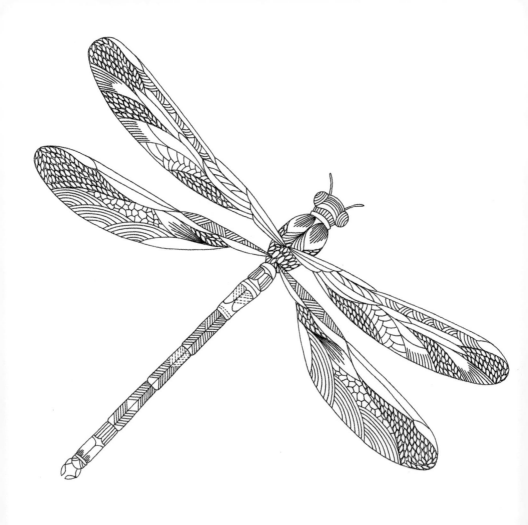

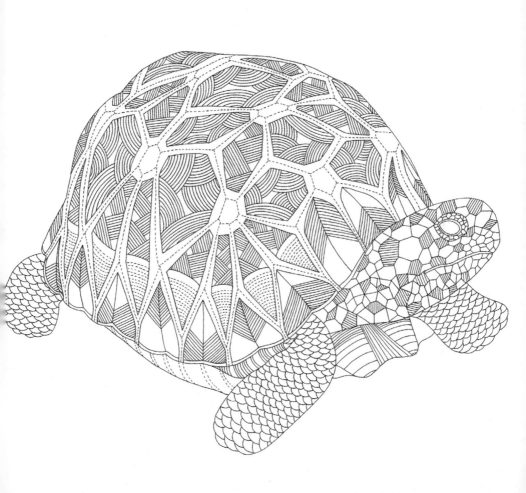

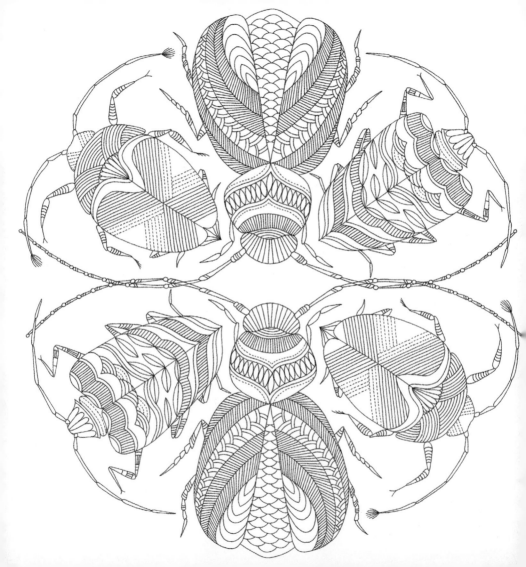

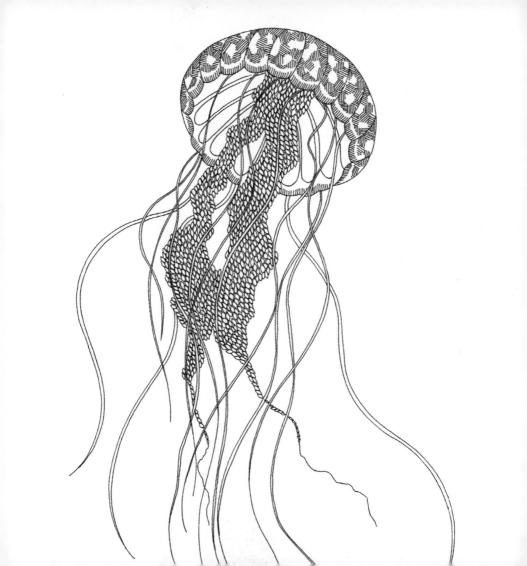

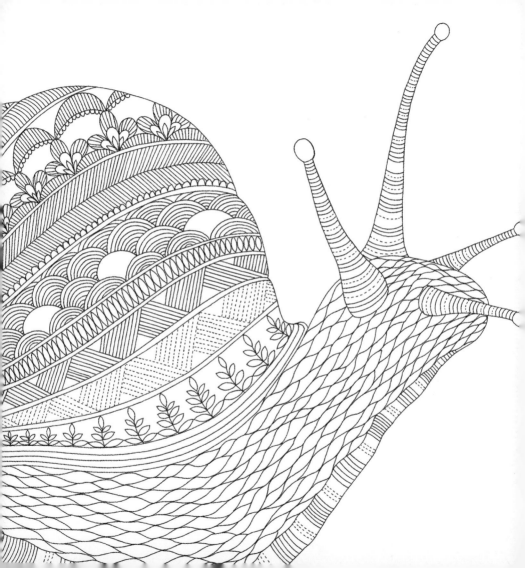

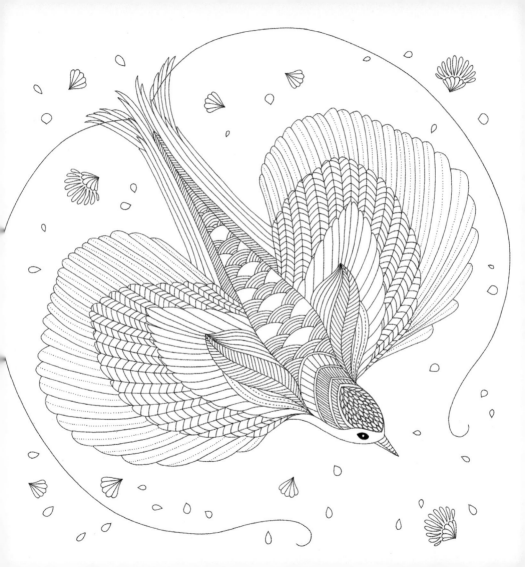

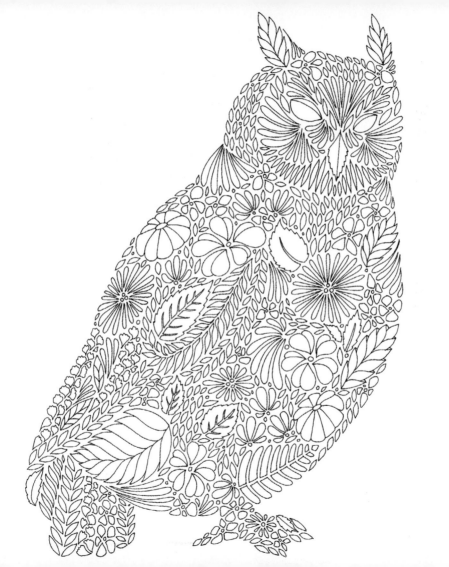

List of creatures in *Animal Kingdom*

For those of you who are curious to know exactly what creatures are featured, here's a list of the illustrations, in the order that they appear in the book.

Octopus

Indian elephant

Damselflies

Butterflies

Moth

Pigeon

Budgie

Raccoon

Red fox

Tropical fish

Moths

Ladybirds

Magpies in the forest

Sea lion

Cockerel

European hare

Tortoise

Woodpeckers

Tropical fish

Grey heron

Flower

Stag

Giraffe

Woodland birds

Beetles

Honey bee

Frogs

Chaffinch

Magpie

Jellyfish

Leaping hare

Rabbit

Butterflies

Ruby-throated hummingbird

Black-capped chickadee

Bumblebee and flowers

White rhinoceros

Gorilla

Toucan

Chameleon

Snake

Birds of paradise

Field mouse

Giraffes

Hippopotamus

Bees and floral pattern

Snail

Honey bees and honeycomb

Flamingo

Peacock

Bird of paradise

Grasshoppers

Blue tit

Pileated woodpecker

European bee-eaters

Brown bear and cub

Ram

Garden birds

Long-eared owl

Create an animal kingdom of your own...

Test your colour palettes…